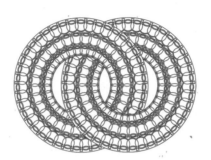

THE LOST NOSTALGIAS

THE
LOST NOSTALGIAS

ESTEBAN RODRÍGUEZ

CAVANKERRY
PRESS

CavanKerry Press Ltd.
Fort Lee, New Jersey
www.cavankerrypress.org

Publisher's Cataloging-in-Publication Data
provided by Five Rainbows Cataloging Services

Names: Rodríguez, Esteban, 1989- author.
Title: The lost nostalgias / Esteban Rodríguez.
Description: Fort Lee, NJ : CavanKerry Press, 2025.
Identifiers: ISBN 978-1-960327-11-6 (paperback)
Subjects: LCSH: Mexican Americans--Poetry. | Family life--Poetry. | Mothers and sons--Poetry. | Fathers and sons--Poetry. | Nostalgia--Poetry. | BISAC: POETRY / American / Hispanic & Latino. | POETRY / Subjects & Themes / Family.
Classification: LCC PS591.M49 R63 2025 (print) | LCC PS591.M49 (ebook) | DDC 811/.54--dc23.

Cover artwork: Coral Sue Black
Interior text design by Natasha Kane
First Edition 2025, Printed in the United States of America

CavanKerry Press is proud to publish the works of
established poets of merit and distinction.

Made possible by funds from the
New Jersey State Council on the Arts, a partner
agency of the National Endowment for the Arts.

CavanKerry Press is grateful for the generous support it
receives from the New Jersey State Council on the Arts, as
well as the following funders:

The Academy of American Poets
Community of Literary Magazines and Presses
National Book Foundation
New Jersey Arts and Culture Renewal Fund
New Jersey Economic Development Authority
The Poetry Foundation

Also by Esteban Rodriguez

Dusk & Dust (2019)
Crash Course (2019)
In Bloom (2020)
(Dis)placement (2020)
The Valley (2021)
Before the Earth Devours Us (2021)
Ordinary Bodies (2022)
Limbolandia (2023)
Lotería (2023)

I don't want to repeat my innocence. I want the pleasure of losing it again.
    —F. Scott Fitzgerald, *This Side of Paradise*

Contents

IV. Secondhand Elegies

I. Old Country Curses

Old Country Curse

Teeth

When my mother would open her mouth,
I'd imagine a set of fossils, yellowed
and misshapen bones lodged in the velvet

desert of her gums. I'd imagine the dentist
she'd visit in Mexico as an archaeologist,
who, while staring down, mirror and drill

in hand, was unsure on how best to clean
and dig them out. And I'd imagine that when
the monotony and loneliness of cleaning a house

became too much, she'd step out onto the porch,
light a cigarette, savor each drag. I never found
those Camels, Lucky Strikes, Marlboros,

never traced anything to a habit other than
that faint smell of smoke clinging to her breath.
But I wanted to believe she was addicted

to the practice; that this, and only this,
was the reason for the rottenness, because
what else but her own body's betrayal

could cause craters to pockmark her molars,
or to flatten her canines, or to coerce her front teeth
to begin to disappear, erasing what enamel she had

left. When her incisors fell off, and I could
no longer imagine that maybe she didn't brush,
or that this was some old country curse—

a generational spell of cavities and plaque—
I'd look away every time she spoke, and without
opening my mouth, run my tongue across my teeth,

feeling the way I felt during grade school once,
when outside, beside a swing set, a bottom chomper
loosened, came off, and all I could think about,

as I held it in my palm, was putting it under
my pillow when I got home, hoping that when
I woke up in the morning, another tooth—whiter,

thicker, no longer crooked—would have
sprouted, eager to grow.

Shave

Nightgowned and hunched
at the sink, my mother says

she's ready, and I wonder
if when I'm done shaving

her last patches of hair, she'll look
in the mirror, sigh with relief,

tell herself how glad she feels
that the curls around her ears

are gone, that she no longer looks—
as she likes to claim—like some sad,

radioactive clown, or like the mangy
dogs that roam the neighborhood,

skulking every lawn. Or will she not
look, leave the bathroom without

saying a word, and on her way
to her room, reflect on how,

decades ago, she made me stand
by the same sink, and after washing

out the gel from my newly
bleached hair, after saying that this

is not how I was raised,
she shaved my head, and to emphasize

the punishment, slapped the back of it,
so I'd remember how not to behave

again, so when I was on my high horse,
convinced I owned the world,

I'd remember how it feels
when what I love is gone.

Bleached

Of course, I didn't listen,
but when my mother saw my hair,
blonder than I had bleached it

before, she didn't curse me out,
didn't say, in that disappointed Spanish
I never learned, that I had ruined

who I really was, unless I wanted
to look like a gringo, because—and this
I assumed she thought but never said—

my skin already looked like one—
pale, and at times—when doused in sunlight
and seen at just the right angle—transparent,

like that of some exotic fish, and like someone
who didn't look as if his parents were
from Mexico, and who much less knew

what it meant to have to pick, at some point
in his life, crops in a field, letting the sun
singe more indifference on his skin,

while knowing that even if this
wasn't the case, he'd still be different,
that wherever he went some would stare,

some would look away.

Dapper

For prom, my mother suggests
my grandfather's suit, confident
the brown pants aren't too wide,

loose, that the sleeves extending
past my hands look as they should,
or will in the coming months, since,

as my mother reminds me again,
my growth spurt is overdue.
And *oh mijo, how chulo you will look,*

how, like my grandfather, I
will command the attention of the room,
and how, on the dance floor,

with my date melting in my arms,
the other girls will wish they were
with me. But when I try it on,

and my mother squeezes me in,
says, *Looks good, Esteban, looks good,*
I know she's feigning happiness,

that really she wants to get rid of
that go-to outfit her father used
for weddings, quinceañeras, barbecues,

of what reminded her of his constant
presence, of the way I guess—
because why not infer a narrative—

he'd come home after work,
and with the suit still on, he'd enter
each of his daughters' rooms,

walk toward their beds, and as a tipsy
silhouette, would hover over them,
not to provide comfort, but as a reminder

that he was always watching,
that even when his body was gone,
his memory would never wear out.

Tongue

Esplain

Thirteen, and already I'd mastered
language, the *shits*, the *fucks*, the *bitches*
and *who the hell gives a crap, goddamn.*

And so why not move into lecture, laugh
when my mother says *esplain*, the x trapped
in the back of her mouth. Why not cut her off,

say, with such authority, *It's explain, Mom.*
Ex-plain. And why not think, when she shrugs it
off and says what she has to say, that she

would never get it, that when she and I
were at a place whose walls and scent felt
governmental, and the person behind

the desk knew only fragments of high school
Spanish, she would again turn to me, expect,
because I knew so much, to make that English

less useless, less harsh.

-ed

Either my father would forget to pronounce it,
or he'd add it where it wasn't needed,

like the one time at dinner when he broke
his silence to tell us about an incident, how one

of his coworkers, a man no older than he was,
dropped some piece of steel from his hand,

grabbed his chest, and began to pant, only my father
didn't say *pant*, but *breatheded. He breatheded*

real hard. And I wondered why he said
this in English, as if doing so would remove

him from the picture, and he wouldn't have to
imagine this happening to him, wouldn't have to

second guess what he carried, how far he carried it,
or what it meant when he was suddenly out

of breath, if he'd have time to think through
each of his regrets, or if he'd enter quickly into

the past tense, be *muerto, dead.*

Beach

On the drive home, my mother says
that she liked that *bitch*, and I know,
even with her sunburnt pronunciation,

that she means *beach*, that the ship
of distinction between the two has long
since sailed. I think of the girls

at school, how *bitch* flows so frequently
from their lips, how when they say it
to each other they mean it as acceptance,

recognition for the group they're in.
But what group does my mother belong to?
Where does she land when it comes to

the words that haven't found refuge
in her mouth, when the *esplain* makes me
want to laugh, when the *congrachoolashuns*

sounds like she's about to have a stroke,
or heart attack, and makes me feel,
unlike the way I felt when I was young,

guilty for thinking this in the first place,
because I know, regardless of what she can
and cannot say, she'll speak with a confidence

I can only hope to convey.

Congratulations

But she wanted to pronounce it all,
say it in the best English she knew.
So when the occasion demanded it

be used—good grades, basketball wins,
graduation—I'd listen to her *con*
and *gra* strung harshly together,

then the *choo* that followed, how it sounded
like she was mocking a sneeze, faking
an oncoming sickness, attempting to get out

of prior commitments. But she committed
to the *la* and *shuns* that came out next,
not the *tion* I remember once, after dinner,

practicing with her—*nation, communication,
humiliation*, words I realize now,
years after this kitchen table scene,

I should have cared less about,
because didn't her attempts count,
didn't her *Congrachoolashuns* mean

what it meant all along?

Herbalife

Pretty soon, I had my own
line to sell—weight loss shakes,

protein bars, drinks for digestive
health. And because I witnessed

my mother—every weekend
at some friend of a friend's house—

secure her own clientele, I branched
off on my own, tried to make a name

for myself, hit the neighborhood
first, hoping some mother or middle-

aged daughter still living at home
would invite me in, see what I had

to offer. But when that didn't work,
and I was left standing in front

of an afternoon of closed doors,
I had to remind myself that I

wasn't selling alarm systems or knives,
but a lifestyle choice, a chance

for someone to better themselves,
which is why the women at my mother's

get-togethers agreed not only to buy
so much, but to sell for her, to believe

that if they push this or that miracle pill,
they too could be their own boss.

Payback

Because pain can make anyone
a different person, I shoved my mother
off me, claimed that this was personal,

that my shoulder—dislocated, loose
like the wheel of a shopping cart—
was her chance to take it out on me,

payback for the socks I never picked up,
for the stacks of dishes I never washed,
for the one time I felt brave, looked her

dead in the face, and talked back.
This was retribution, never mind the bump
in the asphalt that led to my fall,

to the sudden numbness in my arm,
and to how I, like a fugitive, fled
from the bike and ran to the middle

of the yard, where my mother, always ready
for an emergency, led me to the car,
and while whispering what sounded

like spells and prayers, while summoning
the strength to grip my shocked and shaking
body, slammed me sideways against

our van, not once, not twice, but until
my shoulder locked back in place,
and until I felt, because the cure had done

more damage than the cause, that the sting
could be healed if there was someone,
anyone to blame.

Cure

After pickle juice, Gatorade, Sprite,
after prayers and prayer candles placed
in bowls of water beneath the bed,

there was VapoRub, sticky, thick,
plopped like batter in the middle
of your chest. Slowly, my mother spread it,

rubbed the cream from my collarbone
to my ribs. And though she lingered,
made me wonder how uncomfortable

I should feel, I accepted her mind
was somewhere else, that as the VapoRub
disappeared, and she began to utter

a list of chores, she was picturing herself
at a bar, a dance, at a bright place
without a sick son, and without the need

to tend to him, to hum—as she worked
more ointment on her palms—a song
whose lyrics she had long forgot.

II. At the Feet of the Empty-Handed

Home Depot

Even when work was steady,
my father went on the weekends,
stood with his hands in his pockets,
quiet, shivering, though it wasn't

from the cold as much as it was
from anticipation, from the buildup
when more men arrived, and when
a truck passed by, then another,

and another, none of them stopping,
none of them fitting these men's
visions of how they saw their days
going, of being picked out, jumping

onto the back of a truck, and working
all afternoon on some part of a house:
driveway, roof, new additions
to a backyard, or whatever made them

a few bucks, and that when they went
home, they could feel not just like men,
but like fathers who were earning
a living, who wouldn't have to imagine

themselves still in that Home Depot
parking lot, hopeful and waiting.

Biweekly

Two weeks later, and we're at the bank again,
again in line, again waiting as the tellers call up

servers still in uniform, shop owners, secretaries
whose makeup had faded early in the afternoon,

and who—away from anything that required
they maintain an appearance—are not concerned

that their hair is disheveled, that their skirts
are askew, that the Band-Aids, bloodied from

the blisters on their ankles, are flaring from
the backs of their heels. And there are construction

workers, men in grease-stained blue jeans,
paint-smeared shirts, steel toes they shuffle

across the tile, as slow and impatient as my father.
He looks over. They look back. And I understand

from their silence that even if there's mutual respect,
there's also a wariness of the logos on their chests,

of the DH, LG, JD Incorporated, letters that mean
nothing to me, but that to my father equate

with a new Home Depot, Lowe's, with contracts
their bosses vied for, and that if gotten

led to at least another month of work. Slowly, the line
moves forward. My father peeks inside his envelope,

makes sure his name is still on the check,
and I look up, wonder if he's worried the teller

will ask him for some ID he doesn't have, proof
that he earned the money he's requesting in cash.

And maybe this is why he's begun walking into banks
the way the elderly do, mindful of the crowd and commotion,

of the bankers sitting at their desks, of an institution
with computers that hold so much information,

and with believing, as my grandfather used to claim,
that nothing can beat the knowledge that when

you went to bed, what you worked so hard for
was tucked beneath the same place you slept.

Nightcap

Nights my father wasn't home,
I crashed his liquor cabinet,

which wasn't a cabinet at all,
but instead a shelf, a dusty,

darkened space where between
the whiskey, tequila, and rum,

rested a bottle of Belvedere, which,
being the only one my father

never drank, I chugged, feeling,
from what I thought I knew

about vodka, like a Russian villager,
an old and jaded man who needed

to drink to keep his body warm,
only the coldness I suffered

wasn't the weather, but absence,
the void I felt when my father

left home, when after a half-day at work
he refused to bear the same old same old:

stale dinner, novelas, game shows,
the silence my mother made sure

he heard, no matter which room
she was in. And where he went

was anyone's guess, though I imagined
it was more than just a bar, that it

was a spot where his drink was filled
for him, and where when he downed

another round, his throat, unlike mine,
didn't burn, but felt cool, smooth,

felt that every drop was a drop
he was proud he earned.

Hitchhiker

Past the checkpoint,
I spot a man
with a backpack, waving

a rag above his head.
When my father
spots him too, takes

his eyes off the road
to take in this figure
emerging from the bush,

I wonder what he thinks,
if he sees himself in this man,
if he remembers, as I

believe the blank stare
in his face says he does,
his own crossing, how it

wasn't until the third, fourth,
maybe even fifth attempt
that he made it to the river,

and how at the river—
moonlight scarred on
its murky surface—

he didn't think twice before
jumping in, knowing
that he if didn't emerge

a new man, then at least he'd
come out breathing new air,
and that when he walked

farther into this new land,
someone who had made it
was bound to pick him up,

to see him waving by the side
of some road, ready to lend
more than just a hand.

Burro

As old as every finger on my hands,
I'm told I no longer need balloons, confetti,
no more red candy gushing from a torn
piñata's belly, no father tugging the rope,

laughing, taunting, yelling. No, the father
I get now is the father that leads me
into our corral, where I'm gifted an altered
version of a pony he once promised:

a burro tied to a pole, standing with
enough will to let me run my fingers
through its swollen head, its crooked jaw,
then down along its coffee-colored coat

of fur caked in fleas and dust. And as my father
steps back, lifts the Polaroid to his face,
I can't help but think that after I pose,
I'll be made to bound the burro's legs,

to grip the knife that suddenly appears
in my hand, and with a smile I'll feel
the need to own, watch the blood
and aftermath make my father proud.

Requiem

And after my father straps a blade
to its claw, and mumbles what I assume
is the end of a prayer, I wonder

what part of this is real, what sliver of truth
pits him against a figure so eager
to thrust his rooster forward, to let gravity

guide it to the ground, and to watch—
as my father steps back, becomes spectator
and coach—the chaos that ensues,

the *ki-ki-ri-kís*, the stabs, the wounds,
the blood that anoints the blood
already spilled, the way the fighters' necks

droop, until one—fatigued from the blows—
takes a hit and falls headfirst, becoming
a mass of mangled meat and feathers

my father casts his shadow on, nudges
the way I nudge his body on weekend
afternoons, convinced my touch—

calm and sober—will be enough
to make him rise once again.

Rome

Before one project's done, my father
starts the next—front porch, driveway,

a new roof for an unfinished shed.
And within the house, there are unpainted

cabinets, missing tiles and laminate,
a kitchen sink that continues to leak.

Yes, there is more than enough work for him
to complete, and yet, my father can't see

a project through, can't bring himself
to work on one and only one thing

for an afternoon, perhaps because he likes
the way my mother gets after him,

or the way she shakes her head,
or how she'll go for weeks without

speaking, hoping he'll find motivation
in her silence. Or perhaps it's because I

never lend a hand, and to spite me,
he doesn't nail that board, doesn't tighten

that screw, doesn't even out the edges
of a cut plank of wood, because he wants me

to feel some sense of guilt, because he wants
me to know that his version of Rome

will take more than a day to build.

Pride

For days, my father kept his hand
hidden, tucked it at an angle where

it seemed like it wasn't needed,
until my mother became suspicious,

and without warning during dinner,
grabbed his arm, slammed it on the table,

and listened, after he grunted, cursed,
spewed phrases in Spanish I had never

heard, to the details of his accident,
how the brick tore open the top

of his hand, how he thought it would heal
with faucet water, ointment, prayer,

how he worked half-day shifts
through the pain, found new ways

to carry plywood and rebar, hoping,
even when he couldn't move his fingers,

that his body would heal as it healed before,
that he'd never have to ask for help.

Mechanics

Always a brother, an uncle, a friend
of a friend of a friend of the family,
someone who wouldn't charge too much,
owned his own shop, which was really
a dirt driveway, maybe a garage,

or some unused section of a backyard
where he could install new parts,
change the oil, pump Freon, superglue
a bumper back on, or do whatever
he was so skilled at doing to fix any type

of car. He was sometimes young, barely
out of high school, but with a body
already aged by decades beyond his years,
no different from the older mechanics,
who, more often than not, were the ones

my father went to when problems
with the engine became too complex
to figure out. I remember his disappointment
those afternoons, the look as he stood
in front of his truck or my mother's van,

staring, in silence, beneath the hood
as though he were at a funeral, and perhaps,
in his mind, some small part of him was,
a witness to the death of his manliness,
or to that aspect of his ego that caused him

to put away his toolbox, tie a rope or chain
to the front bumper, and haul that vehicle
to the outskirts of town, where we
would pull up at the mechanic's house,
and where I alone would sit in the front

seat, study my father's forced laughter,
his sloppy hand movements, his "I've tried
everything" body language that eased him
into handing over the keys, and that allowed
him to walk back with his head up, confident

that in the right hands, the most broken things
could be repaired.

Abandon

On the shoulder, they rest—
truck, car, van. And all afternoon,
as I drive past each of them,

I wonder why they've been
abandoned, if they had run out
of gas, had a tire blown out,

or if the engine, as personified
as any object, had just given up,
which is what my father said

that night, years ago, he came home
soaked in sweat, and upon taking off
his shirt, revealing slivers of darkness

leeched to his skin, damned his truck,
cursed it out, as if it were a son,
one who after spending weeks

practicing his swing and stance,
struck out, again and again. Yes,
for a moment I thought this

was about me, until, after what felt
like hours passed, I realized
the truck was a metaphor,

that this was about his past,
that when he knew his homeland
was running on fumes, and it

could no longer carry him
on any path, he, like every nomad
before him, had to walk away

from it, and hope that days later,
sun-scorched and less of himself,
he would cross that mythic line,

find a place that would open its doors,
and welcome him home.

Trash

Though I knew he hadn't *left* left,
my father was gone, and in his absence,

my mother refused everything that reminded
her of him: TV, couch, his sweaty side

of the bed. And there were the plates—
of all things—that she refused to touch,

perhaps because of the way he ate off them,
scraping his knife and fork, or licking,

if he had downed some tall boys before,
the chaos of food caked around the edge.

Or perhaps she left them in the cabinets
because she wanted to forget, to pretend

she was never married, that she didn't have
a shotgun wedding, that she lived a life

where the dishes could stay in the sink,
stacked up for weeks, reeking to the point

where she began buying paper plates,
so there was no need to clean,

so when she had enough, she could throw
what she no longer wanted away.

Bury

The club but not the gloves.
The bag, not the balls he picked up,

gazing at them like a new specimen.
No, my father bought nothing else

at the garage sale that day,
and at home, with the club in his hand,

he stood in the middle of the yard,
swung at nothing again and again,

until something within him said
he should hit every empty beer can,

and after sending them into the driveway
or street, he should swing at what

had long been ignored: rusted nails,
chunks of wood, small car parts

my father had tossed, saying,
if only to himself, that he was going

to use them someday, only that day
never came, and instead this one

found him swinging, so suddenly,
harder, harder, hoisting the club

over his head, and with all his strength,
smashing the ground till he made a hole,

one, I believed, where he could bury
if not his anger, then at least his regret—

everything he could have done, every
version of himself he could have been.

III. Backyard Baptisms

Landlocked

Midsummer. The sky's again contused
and cloudless, still dizzy with mirages

heaving on patches of surviving grass,
on scattered heaps of backyard crates,

on the rust-gnawed remains of a Firebird
I dig through. I exhume and lift a carburetor

to my ear, shake it softly like a seashell,
and hear unexpected waves crackling

against themselves. There are hungry seagulls
squatting motionless in the air, cruise ships

horning their way punctually into port,
sunburnt tourists unfolding their bodies

like beach chairs, flinging their foreign laughs
and lingo at the gurgled crash of foam.

Like all things imaginary though, this scene
wasn't built to hold, so I grip the serrated sides

more maraca-like, nauseate the shore
till my hands begin to ache, till the sea

regurgitates archipelagos of thrown plastic,
dead fish and sailors, legends of shipwrecks

the moon-drunk tides have anchored to asterisks
of sand; every message-in-a-bottle backwashed

like an oil spill. I bend down, pick them up,
and like God after every plague, every flood,

survey this altered version of my backyard.
What is paradise but the history we never see,

themed hotels, glossy strips of restaurants,
and palm trees? An island easier to picture

than this accidental scrapyard, stacked
and used-car parts I try to salvage, dragging

out slabs of jagged steel as if they were shark
victims, as if I were here to save them,

to bring back a world I imagine
one day will believe in me.

Quinceañera

August. The plains sacrifice themselves
to a humid sunset. The sky nibbles the edges
of evening, and all that glitters glitters

from the white and wrinkled folds of a rented
dress; my barefoot, fifteen-year-old cousin
standing like a mannequin in the middle

of the driveway, heels in hand, tiara planted
on her head, clouds of caliche hugging
her skin, because there is no runway here

made of marble or cement, no postreception
view better than the picnic table where I sit.
I watch beads of expired hairspray fade

down her neck, seep through the cracked
and clay-colored pores of blush curdled
into sweat. And as the patterns on my cousin's

face begin to melt, I know I'm witnessing
the same rite my aunts and mother once endured,
a chapter I'll never reach, since all traditions

are one-sided, and since the moon, yawning
into importance, grants permission for gnats
to swirl above me, to become the only crown

I'll ever be allowed to keep.

Bluebonnets

Rest stop as godsend. As a chance
to smell the asphalt for what it truly is.

So I wander toward the bluebonnets
scattered by the trash bins. Spring's

fevered wind warms my face, and I
kneel to swipe away the scattered trash,

the faded candy wrappers planted
loosely like bouquets, the crumpled

soda cans rendered into an accidental
Stonehenge, and the greasy paper bags

tangled on their fuzzy stems. Abandoned
for years by lack of shade, their heat-

and insect-gnawed petals chalk inside
my hands, cling to my grip like Velcro,

and I contemplate whether I should pluck
one out, play a smaller version of God

and orchestrate their exodus to a different
ground, because like black sheep ostracized

from their flock, they're the batches
not even the hill country wants, withered

strays not pictured on postcard racks,
plaques or key chains, family photo

backdrops, or souvenirs any tourist
would ever care to take, since they

sway with the pulse of the interstate's
indifference, and mirror the sunflowers

my window, not even a few minutes ago,
blurred into a brushstroke of flames—

that backseat flash I placed my fingers on,
traced a path along all day, until they too

became what could only be admired
from a distance, and these bluebonnets

emerged like a truth too harsh to accept,
a parched and roadside anatomy slipping

from my fingertips, as they now shift out
of my silhouette's frame, and buckle further

into silence, like hitchhikers who've lost
their will to turn back and wave.

Rain

Above the windowsill, the unemployed sky
yawns to a mood fit for the middle of July,

smuggles another horde of clouds from
the swollen gulf. With what's already

been amassed, they become billboards
of overcast, bruised and lethargic advertisements

for rain. The air thickens, grazes the distant
sagebrush with new definitions of dampness,

and I remember that I've long since accepted
the sun's ancestral bronzing, the way it tones

my flesh to the density of callus and brands
my shadow to the ground so my body can't escape.

My skin thirsts for that darkness huddling
on the plains, for that climate that suddenly

acknowledges the landscape's prayers, begins
to bead my window with broken rosaries

of condensation, a drizzled illusion I enter.
Inside, I wander the hypothetical heart of a city,

the alleyways and districts, the cross-hatched
street corners where the underground labyrinths

of steam rise like incense toward the fading
rows of streetlamps, and brush against my legs

like a stray dog no longer afraid of sidewalk
traffic. Evening's extended prologue, jaundiced

with uncertainty, tosses its showers along
the pavement, then veils the skyline with

an insomnia of fog and anonymity, with
a sense that I can keep everything at its periphery

and still sustain a narrative long enough to suspend
my daily exodus of sweat, to erase the generational

layers of salt glazed across my limbs,
and watch as the rain decorates the horizon with

clichés of lightning, thunder, with a chant
ready to fertilize its long and ceremonial downpour.

Shed

Gnat- and ant-infested, the shed stands
slanted on a mound out back, its sagging
sheets of steel warped by brush that's pushed

its way in, by waist-high weeds tangled
on loosened bolts, on slabs of concrete
I slowly step over, like this were some

ancient ruin, and I the archeologist awed
by artifacts of shovels, rakes, by hoes
and coiled water hoses, by crooked shelves

lined with jars of nails, kerosene lamps,
and bags of potting soil that were used
when it was once possible to garden the yard.

I push farther in, and when I realize that all things
are purposeless before they become purposeful,
I begin to drag out what tools I can,

so that generations from now, when the world
is less of itself, someone can stumble onto this,
know at least one person cared.

Broma

Of course, I heard the joke before,
how Mexicans like barbecuing in the park,

how they hold birthdays and weekend
get-togethers there, claim a table and pit

and watch it fill with uncles, cousins, aunts,
with family who haven't been spoken to

in months. And when my roommate asks
if it's true, if my childhood consisted

of such a scene, I forget for a moment
the privilege of ignorance, think of a table

full of birthday cake, plates, drinks, think
of how I was once escorted beneath a tree,

and how after being tossed a broken
broomstick, I was given permission

to hit that rainbow-colored piñata, again
and again, and to never once think that

when the pony broke open, spilled its guts
of chocolate bars, lollipops, and unlabeled

candy, the reward on the ground
wouldn't be mine to take.

Mojado

During recess once, I heard a boy
joke about another boy, heard him mock

his accent, make fun of how dark his skin was
compared to those who'd gathered around.

I laughed, but wondered why I thought
I had to laugh, or why this boy would say this

when in fact he was darker than the boy
he joked about, or why I and those around me

didn't point this out, but gave him a pass,
let him say, Mojado. *He looks like a mojado,*

and let everyone forget they didn't have fathers
or grandfathers who had crossed the river once,

who decades before stood in front of that
uncertain water, and as the sun further darkened

their skin with synonyms for "other,"
had no choice but to dive in, to believe that when

they emerged on new land, they'd be just the same
as everyone else.

Pool

Though I worked on my abs all spring,
I took off my shirt reluctantly, aware

of the girls from school sunbathing
in the corner, of how beneath their shades

they were probably scanning for new flings,
for someone whose heart they could break

over the summer. I hoped I was one of them,
that when I jumped in, the water and sun

glistened off my skin, and for a moment
I'd be the embodiment of their dreams,

or at least of a boy who had less acne
on his back, who didn't hunch, who time

and time again didn't have to push
his glasses up, who didn't fit descriptions

of someone who must bear joke after insult
after prank, but instead dishes them out,

because he knows that no matter how deep
he sinks beneath literal and metaphorical

waters, his body, or some part of it,
will find a way to rise up.

Throw Down

With rumors in every room,
I learn who wants to throw down
with who, that tomorrow,

or the next day or the next,
I will face an enemy I didn't know
I had. And so, I go home,

raid my mother's jewelry box,
put on every ring she owns,
and in my room, after I convince

myself how angry I should feel,
I begin punching the wall,
over, over, and over again,

until the bleeding starts,
and my knuckles become numb,
and I imagine this is the way

my father feels, not just fatigued
when he comes home from work,
but defeated, less of himself,

ready to take out what he bottled
all day on the nearest wall,
or on a lamp, a chair, or on a cheek

that sometimes happens to be mine,
or that sometimes, when I'm
at a distance watching him,

is my mother's. And I imagine,
knowing that I shouldn't,
that if I'm as successful

as my father is, my opponent
will limp to the corner, and after
the crying stops, and silence swells

his throat, he will look at me,
like my mother looks at my father,
and accept that when two bodies

are thrust together, one is bound to lose.

All-State

Not a god, but a god among us,
a center who runs the court,

meets the pass, spins, dunks, revels
in the cheers and awe, while we

slow to take out the ball, try to compose
ourselves, try not to think about

the score, how we'll feel with another loss,
or if, when the game is over

and the season winds down, any of this
will matter at all, if years from now

when we think of the center—remember
how during practice we shoved him,

shouted, shit-talked, and tried to avoid
being posted up—we'll be content

where life has taken us, with knowing
that in college he warmed the bench,

transferred a year after, then dropped out,
and that when we go out, grab wings

and a beer, we see him alone at the bar,
watching the game, rooting, silently,

for those who made it to the top.

Blows

One guards the door. Another
lends the wall his shadow.
I move toward the one cursing

softly in Spanish, egging the boys
in the middle on. And as they take
the bait, thrust forward, blend

their limbs into an awkward blur,
and bump, between each attempt
at a punch, into the urinals, the stalls,

I remember you, your arms,
the certainty of your nails, grip,
palms; how I learned that skin,

under pressure, force, has no incentive
to stay intact, and that the cuts
speckled across my wrists, neck,

jaw, wouldn't reveal their pain
till I was alone. The boys slip
on piss. Gravity pulls on their waists,

and when they hit the ground—
back and elbows breaking their fall—
I too am back on the floor:

your thighs squeezing my ribs,
your forearm across my face,
muffling, as you push down,

the laughs that turn into grunts,
which you interpret, even as
they deepen, as a sign for you

to go on, to continue this imagined
match, and to watch me struggle
beneath your weight, knowing

that if I was on top, slapping
your hands, stuffing the words back
inside your mouth, I too wouldn't allow

the momentum to stop.

Siphon

Though I wasn't sure where the cords
led to, what source was feeding the connection,

or if the black box propped between the picture
frames on the TV stand did indeed fall from

the back of a pickup truck—leaving my father
to recover it, explain why he brought another one

to the house—I never questioned where the cable
came from so long as the channels extended

to my room, gave me my dose of Nickelodeon,
Kenan & Kel, *Legends of the Hidden Temple*,

reruns I watched again, again, learning their adventures,
dialogues, mannerisms, how the problems throughout

each show seemed so American, and how the characters
solved them just as such, meaning solutions were found

in half an hour, meaning that meaning was composed
of double entendres, innuendos, puns, a laugh track

that helped drive the plot, and commercial breaks
for Fruit Loops, Slim-Fast, Cinnamon Toast Crunch,

night after night of things I found myself wanting,
asking for in the aisles of Wal-Mart, sneaking

into the cart with the same urgency I'd grip
the remote, pull the covers up, and remembering

that the doors were never meant to be locked, watch
the shadows that passed behind it: my mother's

nightgowned legs, my father's cement-stained boots,
those Rorschach-shifting strides that drew the focus

away from the gauze of static, or the movies on Showtime,
Cinemax, those distorted bodies on top of one another,

whole scenarios I placed myself in, while trying
to distinguish the shapes on screen, knowing

there wouldn't be another chance till the weekend,
and that if the card wasn't reprogrammed, I'd have to

wait till my father came across a new one,
or till I again settled for *Fresh Prince, Friends,*

The Tonight Show where after the first celebrity guest,
the laughter and music began sounding

like my mother's voice, warm and safe enough
to go to bed.

IV. Secondhand Elegies

Rave

But instead of jumping,
letting strobe lights and sweat
christen my face, body,

I think of my parents,
how before they made it
to this country, they were packed

in such dark and impossible
spaces: the bed of a pickup,
a motel room off a highway,

the shade beneath a bush
in the middle of a field, farm,
desert. And there was the back

of a truck, one that carried them
and people like them to the next
point of their journey, and that,

regardless of what air seeped
through its cracks and crevices,
was still too tight to breathe,

to feel nothing short of having
their throats clenched, squeezed,
of having no choice but to believe—

like I believe the more I dance
in this once-abandoned building—
that even if their bodies want to quit,

they must push through the night,
pray that when they wake up
in the morning, they'd have made it

safely to the other side.

Narratives

In past versions, Abuelo shook his head,
said, without moving his lips, that he
was disappointed in my mother,

that he thought girls her age shouldn't
stay out past twelve, hell, even ten.
And though in these versions he walks away,

leaves the conversation for another day,
in this one my tipsy mother suddenly tells,
she was dragged out of her bed by her hair,

beaten in the middle of the floor,
and told that if she wanted to be a *puta*
to be a *puta* somewhere else.

Isn't this how stories go? Aren't narratives
always changed? Doesn't the teller hide
the truth at first, then, when they feel they have

the right to heal, peel back the surface,
reveal every detail, every second of pain.
And don't some exaggerate as well,

feel the need to up the stakes, like my uncle,
who when he talks about the hard time
he did, means his one night in jail.

Or like my aunt who after stubbing
her toe, spoke for weeks about gangrene,
amputation, prosthetic legs, and life

in a wheelchair. Or perhaps like me
when I tell my mother that the bruises
on my neck aren't hickeys at all,

but the aftermath of mosquito bites,
or of bites from a new species of bug
I tried to fend off, swiping the air,

cursing them out, sure that as they attacked,
attacked, attacked, I'd give them hell
before they left a mark.

Stains

On carpets, rugs, across the floors
and countertop. And there were the stains
that grew with the house: oil splatter
on the kitchen wall, late-night coffee

on the couch's arm, that *carne* grease
my mother never cleaned up,
not because she didn't want to,
not because it didn't pain her when

she wiped the table down, ignored
the spot, but to see if my father ever
would. He never did, and when I
got to high school, and the grease

had the shape and smell of mold,
I thought every clump, spill,
every pool of liquid that had hardened
was a grudge my parents held,

or perhaps was just a reminder
that some part of them had given up,
that they realized regardless
of how old they got, something

would always be stained, because
cleanliness was a myth, a belief
not even God could maintain.

Baptismal

Some days, the water wouldn't work,
or at least that's the phrase my mother used
when the city shut it off, when again,

unknown to her, I'd watch, after school,
the city worker sneak into the corner of our yard,
open the meter box, work his hands,

and wrench on the valve. At night,
my father—after explaining to my mother,
that his check wouldn't come for another week—

would let his frustration out by sitting
in his truck, listening, with the windows
halfway down, to albums on pirated CDs,

and singing every now and then the verse,
the chorus, the one line that embodied everything
he thought he would one day be, not the man

who had to go back in and watch his wife
with their children filling up a bucket
in the shower with what water remained,

because there was no way, as her sighs and head
shakes said, that she was going to bed without
washing her body, without feeling she had cleansed

at least some of her stay-at-home skin.
And unlike my father, who walked away,
opened the fridge convinced that sticking

his head in was the same thing as a shower,
my mother sat my sister and me in the middle
of the tub, and in between scrubbing our chest

and arms with soap, she dipped a plastic cup
into the bucket, and poured the cold, cold water
onto our heads, humming what sounded like a prayer,

one that if she repeated enough, would atone
for all her sins.

Vet

Before the blindness, wheelchair,
before the heavy cough and phlegm
caked on the sides of his mouth,

he had his silence, cigarettes,
had his nights alone in the kitchen,
until I walked in, restless and too aware

that when morning came, my mother
would take us home, forgive my father,
and accept him as part of our family again.

Before Abuelo acknowledged me, sighed,
and finished his advice with head shakes
and stares, he'd take a drag, blow rings

of smoke, watch them linger in the air,
and then, as though he were actually there,
describe his time in Vietnam. *The napalm,*

he'd say. *The napalm was everywhere.*
And yes it was, and yes I knew he was lying,
that if he wasn't losing grip on reality,

he was trying—with details of blood
and gore—to make me feel better,
to say that it could always be worse,

that I should look past all of this,
the way he can sit there, look past the men
that died in his arms, the limp bodies

he carried back to camp, and which he
and other men stood around, trying not to cry,
and in between every *Fuck* and *Goddamn,*

lamenting their lives with packs of Camel,
Newport, Lucky Strike, with a sense
that this—if nothing else—was proof

time was on their side.

Yellow Pages

Deadweight, the yellowed Yellow Pages
lie stacked to the splintered windowpane.

My mother, nightgowned and always
framed in the present tense, urges me

to grab some, help her create, rearrange,
replace the coffee tables, and turn them

into towers of telephone numbers, names;
another listing of family and friends

already inscribed into scrolls inside
our heads, and which unlike the "system,"

as my mother feels the need to claim,
don't have to be counted again,

again mailed to our doorstep, torn
of its shrink-wrap, opened to look up

what column we've been categorized in,
and knowing that even though my mother

does page through it when trying to find
a florist, bakery, a business to help her

with whatever day-to-day business
she occupies her stay-at-home time with,

this updated directory will be recycled
for other purposes: a rag, a stand, a coaster,

paper towels to cover the spread of dog piss,
an object to remind the view how the use

of things dwindles in its frequency,
becomes a timepiece, a relic, a bounded

cemetery of advertising and addresses,
and a prop on stage at the school auditorium,

where once assembled and seated, I
and a grade school gradeful of faces

watched a group of muscled men hoist
a stack of yellow pages, squat at the knees,

and squeeze their hands around them,
then twist and pull one end from the other,

because sometimes, when word play
has been exhausted, any attempt at meaning

becomes more meaningful the moment
it's ripped down the middle.

Feet

With feet too cracked, cut, and calloused
to plant, pivot, bend, my grandfather sits
enthroned on his La-Z-Boy all day, draped

in the TV's blue sunset, in that soda-scented
leather reclined in just the right frame,
that I imagine it as an execution chair,

and my grandmother the executioner, cinching
a rubber-band noose around his bicep.
Her needle pierces the vein, pumps it

with a dose of chemicals I still don't understand.
But he doesn't curl his spine the way I do mine
when I see this, doesn't squeal or flinch, barely

realizes something's punctured the folds
of his jellyfish flesh, blind to the roughness
of my grandmother's hands, to that daily feed

of sugar-white liquid coursing through a body
where memories of my younger weight exist,
where my legs are upright again, and every

piggyback ride lives in the present tense. Now,
not even clumps of Vaseline can keep his pores
awake, rejuvenate his soles, give him energy

to flex, take another step, put on the wool socks
I put on for him as he naps again, and as I again
begin to feel like a two-face accomplice,

a rogue assistant, a grandson sneaking around
his grandmother's actions, aware that even if
I can carry him, haul his childlike skeleton

to the door, he'll have to reacquaint himself
with a world he no longer knows.

Elegy

Sunken, stained, speckled with remains
of what we drank and ate on nights we shunned
the kitchen table, the sofa now rests propped
against our backyard fence, where my father,

after hauling it with the strength and sentiment
fit for caskets, struggles to push it over,
to get every inch of its worn, ripped,
and paisley-patterned body into the alley.

By the clothesline, my mother watches,
arms crossed, head lowered, her posture weak
and ceremonial, as though she were looking back
on every party, every unplanned gathering

where hordes of people sat, mingled,
did what guests were supposed to do,
much the way that I did what I had to on afternoons
when she and my father slipped out of view,

left me alone with a girl. My father pushes.
The chain-link teeth dig into its arms,
and as he shoves it with his shoulder,
and my mother mumbles something mournful

in Spanish, I recall the way I, still in a trance
after my girl would leave, would smell the spot
where she sat, trying to relive the moment,
or at least the feeling that this could be called

a moment, because regardless if I couldn't,
if I just sat there—eyes closed, hands caressing
the pillows—there were certain things this sofa kept,
and others that without moments like these

would have been forgotten: the evenings
my mother, father, and I, exhausted from
the summer heat, rested glued to the TV's music
and laughter—our bodies slumped against each other,

melting into that frayed and familiar fabric.

Golden Corral

Once inside, we crowd the meatloaf,
mashed potatoes, pizza, squeeze between
the coleslaw and Salisbury steak,

between the bowls of Jell-O, ice cream,
pudding that spills onto the okra that spills
onto the beans that spill onto the tray

we slip onto a table still wet from the rag
used to clean the spilled food left
from the families before us, families

that ignored the crumbs on the carpet,
the traffic of fathers, mothers, children—
all dressed in their Sunday best—going back

for seconds, returning with salads anointed
in mountaintops of croutons and dressing,
or with sliced turkey, ham, with fish filet,

lasagna, pulled pork, cold pasta, with specials
that last for months, or with the two-for-ones
courtesy of the coupons my mother collected,

unashamed to use what's free, because why
should we not, why pretend this isn't more
than just lunch, or that we won't regret

the drumsticks, pot roast, and ribs we'll leave
on our plates, won't wish we had added
to our beautiful, beautiful waste.

Piggy

On nights my father slept on the couch,
my mother, in nothing but a nightgown,
paced across my room, mumbling the few curses
in Spanish I knew, and brushing her wet,

tangled hair with the palms of her hands,
until, after some sort of solace was found,
she settled at the foot of my bed, pulled back
the blanket, and held my feet so she could take

the piggies to the market. I'd try to hold still,
lock my ankles, dig my heels into the sheets,
and as she served the middle one roast beef,
I'd look down, catch a glimpse of her bare feet:

dry, cracked, callused, succumbing, quicker
than the rest of her body, to what she couldn't find
a way to fight off or balance, and to what years
later became cuts refusing to scab, fungus spilling

from her cuticles, ulcers as sore and swollen
as the punctures from the stray nails my father—
after walking the chaos of a new foundation—
would sometimes endure. And when he'd take off

his boots in the living room, my mother would rush
to his side, remove his socks, douse lotion
on his soles, and stuff his mouth with rounds
of expired pills, so the blood in his foot

would flow, so she wouldn't have to wiggle
any piggy home.

Home

Then, after a decade of a house
on cinder blocks, of empty lots,
chained dogs, of a darkness the crooked

streetlights could neither convince
nor force to move out, my family moves
to a new neighborhood—not the suburbs

I'd seen on TV or imagined when I
eavesdropped on adults, but a series
of houses that looked, no, felt close enough.

I remember the first night
I was there, how my father—
worrier, sleepwalker—stood outside

in the yard, surveyed the field adjacent
to the neighborhood, and for what seemed
like hours, gazed at, stared, looked

in every synonym that showed
he was content with where he was,
that a decade of construction sites,

sixty-hour work weeks, and of bearing
the bright beatings from the sun had finally
paid off, and this, this three-bedroom,

two-bath, this finished driveway
and thick green lawn, yes,
this was the best reward.

Acknowledgments

Many thanks to the editors of the following magazines and journals in which some of these poems first appeared:

Alien Magazine: "Rave"
Boudin: "Bury" and "Throw Down"
Hayden's Ferry Review: "Siphon"
The Indianapolis Review: "Baptismal"
Jarfly Magazine: "Bluebonnets"
Midway Journal: "Abandon," "Hitchhiker," and "Requiem"
Parhelion Literary Magazine: "Home Depot," "Nightcap,"
    "Payback," and "Shave"
Poetry Is Currency: "Biweekly" and "Landlocked"
Psaltery and Lyre: "Quinceañera"
Twyckenham Notes: "Bleached" and "Pride"
Variant Literature: "Teeth"

Thank you to Gabriel Cleveland and everyone at CavanKerry Press for taking a chance on this collection. Special thank you to Baron Wormser for his invaluable editorial insight. Thank you to Stephanie and the feedback and love that she provided. And lastly, thank you, reader.

CavanKerry's Mission

A not-for-profit literary press serving art and community, CavanKerry is committed to expanding the reach of poetry and other fine literature to a general readership by publishing works that explore the emotional and psychological landscapes of everyday life, and to bringing that art to the underserved where they live, work, and receive services.

Other Books in the Notable Voices Series

An Apron Full of Beans: New and Selected Poems, Sam Cornish
The Poetry Life: Ten Stories, Baron Wormser
BEAR, Karen Chase
Fun Being Me, Jack Wiler
Common Life, Robert Cording
The Origins of Tragedy & Other Poems, Kenneth Rosen
Apparition Hill, Mary Ruefle
Against Consolation, Robert Cording

This book was printed on paper from responsible sources.

The text of *The Lost Nostalgias* was set in Futura PT, a versatile and contemporary geometric sans-serif.